TABLETOP TIPSTERS

Easy Mealtime Manners for Kids

Good Manners
Kids Stuff Press℠

By Leslie A. Susskind

Another Kids' and parents, too! Book

This book is an original publication of Good Manners Kids Stuff Press.

Design by Kecia Crowl

For information regarding permission, write to:
Good Manners Kids Stuff Press
Attention: Permissions Department
640 Vassar Road, Strafford, PA 19087

ISBN 10   0-9824744-6-6
ISBN 13   978-0-9824744-6-4

Interested in more good manners books and products? Please visit us at:
www.goodmannerskidsstuff.com and www.goodmannerskidsstuffpress.com
Because good manners might just make the world a better place!™

TABLETOP TIPSTERS

It's easy to learn your table manners when the Tabletop Tipsters show you just what to do.

They know table manners *best* because they're on placemats, used on tables *every* day.

Did you know Table Manners start
right at the beginning, even *before* you eat?
Here's your first tip from Bailey:

Bailey helps Mom set the table, and puts everything in its place:

cup

fork

napkin

plate

knife

spoon

Of course, before you come in for dinner or if you're helping Mom, you'll always want to do what Sammy does:

Sammy washes his hands to clean off the sand.

Now it's time to sit down,
and do what Katie does:

When her Tea Party starts,
Katie sits down
and puts her napkin
on her lap.

Next, see what Danny does
before he starts eating:

Danny's really hungry, but he waits until his family sits down and gives thanks before he starts to eat.

Once you start eating,
there are just a few more
easy table manners tips to follow.
Here's what Teddy does:

Instead of reaching across the table for a piece of pizza at his Birthday Party, Teddy asks his friend to please pass him a slice.

And, here's what Bailey does:

Bailey remembers not to talk
when his mouth is
full of dog biscuits,
and to chew with
his mouth closed.

And, here's how Sammy acts:

Sammy tries a little bite of Brussels sprouts. He doesn't like them, but he keeps his opinion to himself.

It's good to stay tidy.
Look how Katie keeps
herself clean:

Katie uses her fork and spoon (not her fingers) and wipes her hands and mouth on her napkin.

And, Danny knows:

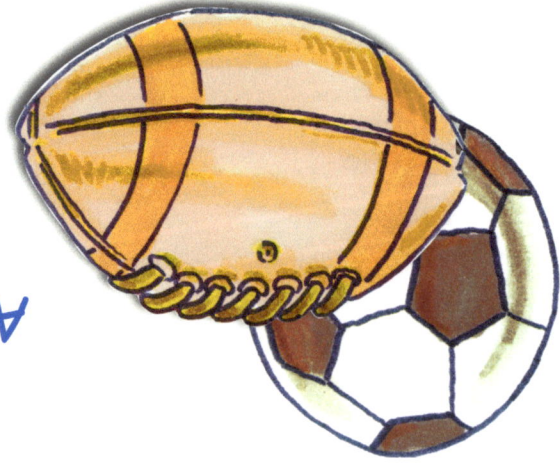

Sometimes it's hard to sit still, but Danny tries his best to stay put while he's eating.

Back at Teddy's party:

Teddy and his friends
are having lots of fun.
His mom reminds them
to use their indoor voices.

Bailey probably shouldn't be doing this in his bowl:

Bailey's mashing up his carrots and peas. Dad reminds him not to play with his food.

And, Sammy remembers:

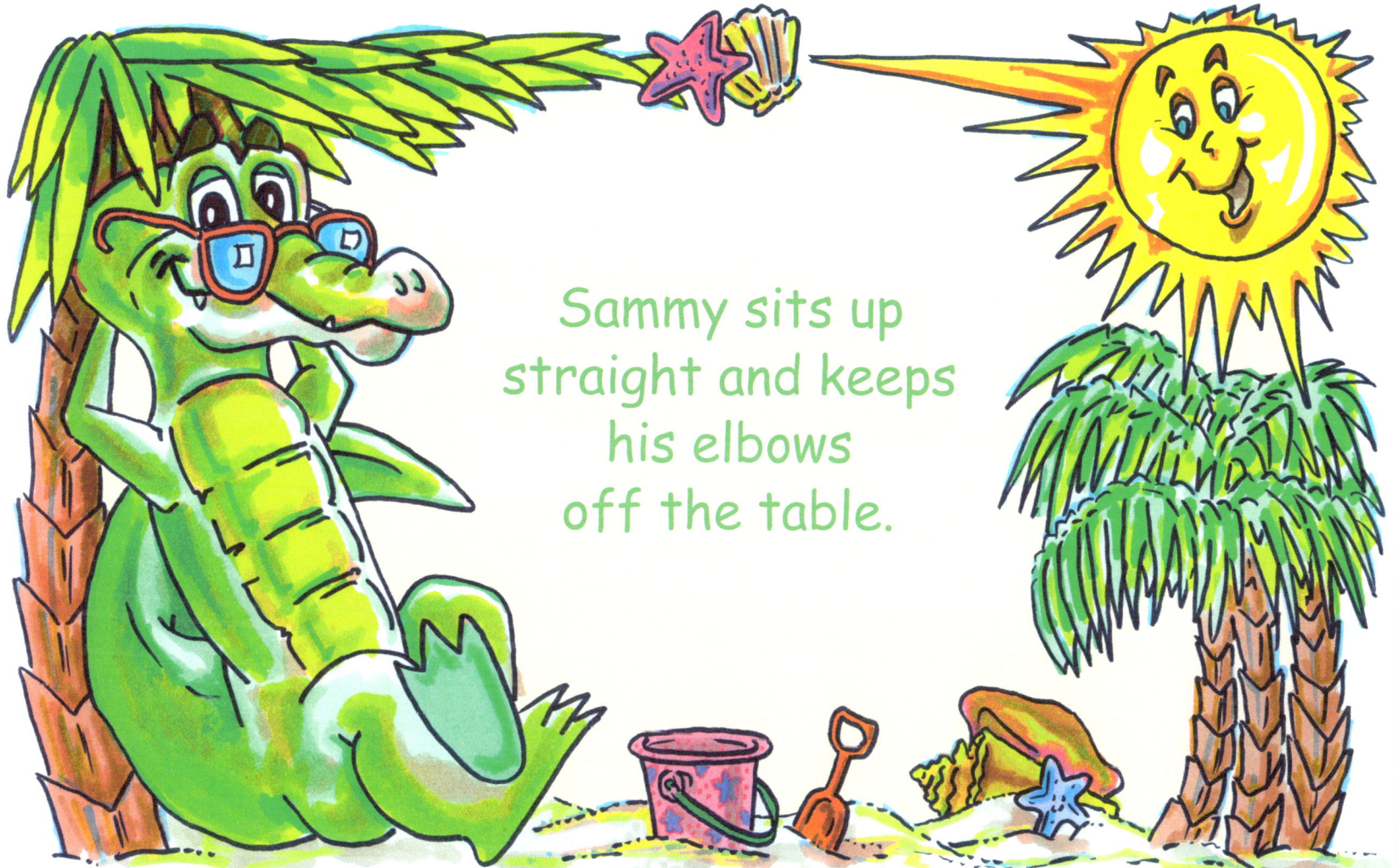

Sammy sits up straight and keeps his elbows off the table.

Oops, Katie's embarrassed :

At her Tea Party,
Katie suddenly burps!
"Excuse me,"
she apologizes.

Now we're finished eating,
and there are just a couple
of table manners tips to go.
Danny knows what comes next:

"May I be excused?"
Danny asks
when dinner's over.

Teddy knows what
he should say, too:

"Thank you for my party
and making my cake,"
Teddy says to Mom
when the party is over.

And the very last tip from Bailey:

Bailey helps clean up the table once dinner's finished.

YOUR TABLE MANNERS TIPS FROM THE TABLETOP TIPSTERS:

Help set
the table

Wash
my hands

Put my napkin on my lap
when I sit down

Wait until everyone
sits down before
I start eating

Don't reach across
the table; and make
sure to say "please"
and "thank you"

Don't talk with my
mouth full or chew
with my mouth open

Don't be rude

Use my fork,
spoon and napkin

Stay in my seat

No burping

Use my indoor voice

Ask if I may
be excused

Don't play
with my food

Say "thank you"
to the cook

Sit up and
keep my elbows
off the table

Help clean up

Good Manners Kids Stuff℠

Because good manners just might make the world a better place!℠

Danny's Table Manners Tip

Danny's a busy boy who has lots of things he wants to do – but he always asks "May I be excused?" when he is finished eating.

Katie the Doll's Table Manners Tip

At her Tea Parties, Katie always keeps her napkin on her lap and uses her fork and spoon when she eats – not her fingers.

Sammy Gator's Table Manners Tip

Before he sits down at the dinner table, Sammy *always* cleans off the sand by washing his hands.

Teddy Bear's Table Manners Tip

At his Birthday Party, Teddy knows it's not polite to reach for his cake – he asks Mom to "Please" pass it to him instead.

Bailey Puppydog's Table Manners Tip:

When Bailey sets the table, here's where he puts everything:

napkin fork plate knife spoon cup

Get the placemats featured in Tabletop Tipsters!
Visit www.GoodMannersKidsStuff.com

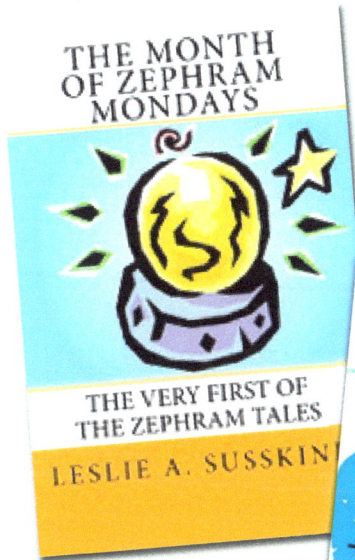

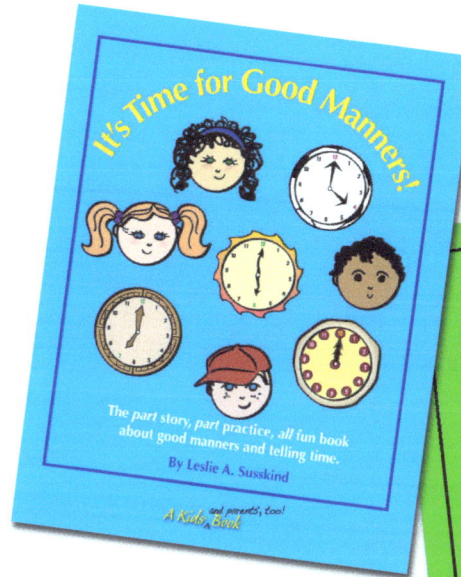

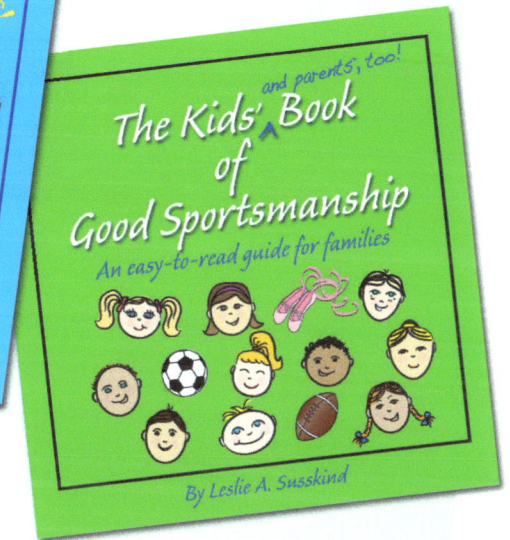

Leslie Aurandt Susskind has worked for years
in advertising and marketing and is excited
to finally be living her life-long dream:
writing children's books!

A busy mom, Leslie lives with her husband, Bill,
and two daughters outside of Philadelphia, Pennsylvania,
where she runs Good Manners Kids Stuff and
its publishing company, Good Manners Kids Stuff Press.

Leslie is also the author of
"The Kids' (and parents', too!) Book of Good Sportsmanship,"
"It's Time for Good Manners!" and the middle grade fantasy novel,
"The Month of Zephram Mondays."
She hopes you'll check with your favorite online retailers, local
bookstores and Good Manners Kids Stuff Press for
more of her books coming soon, including
"The Tale of Time Warp Tuesday," the second of the Zephram Tales.

www.GoodMannersKidsStuffPress.com

www.GoodMannersKidsStuff.com

www.LeslieSusskind.com

www.ingramcontent.com/pod-product-compliance
Lightning Source LLC
Chambersburg PA
CBHW042101040426
42448CB00002B/97